Gra... mons'
H... ook

R D Symons

Grandfather Symons' Homestead Book

Western Producer Prairie Books
Saskatoon, Saskatchewan

Western Producer Prairie Books
Saskatoon, Saskatchewan

Copyright © 1981 by Hope Symons
Western Producer Prairie Books
Saskatoon, Saskatchewan

Cover and book design by GDL

Edited by Candace Savage

Publication of this book has been assisted by the Canada Council and Saskatchewan Arts Board

Printed and bound in Canada
by Modern Press ⟨⟩ Saskatoon, Saskatchewan

Western Producer Prairie Books publications are produced and manufactured in the middle of western Canada by a unique publishing venture owned by a group of prairie farmers who are members of Saskatchewan Wheat Pool. Our first book in 1954 was a reprint of a serial originally carried in *The Western Producer,* a weekly newspaper serving western Canadian farmers since 1923. We continue the tradition of providing enjoyable and informative reading for all Canadians.

Canadian Cataloguing in Publication Data
Symons, R. D. (Robert David), 1898-1973.
    Grandfather Symons' homestead book

    Includes index.
    ISBN 0-88833-082-0

    1. Frontier and pioneer life — Prairie
Provinces — Juvenile literature. I. Title.
FC3242.S95   j971.2'02   C82-091013-9
F1060.9.S95

Contents

Introduction

Whether you live in the eastern, the western, or the central part of Canada, your grandparents may well have grown up on homesteads in the West. They were youngsters in the pioneer days, a time which seems ages ago to you but is still only yesterday to them.

So you must have enjoyed hearing them talk about the old days and about their parents — your *great*-grandparents. You may have heard stories of the long miles that Great-Grandfather traveled by wagon or buggy, of how he plowed with oxen, of stooking, hauling stones, and a thousand and one other jobs which had to be done when our prairie West was young.

You will have heard, also, of Great-Grandmother cooking whole heaps of food for the hungry harvest gangs, of milking cows, tending the garden, and feeding the ducks and chickens.

You may have thought what fun it must all have been, what with the new colts and calves in the spring; the wild strawberries in the summer; the golden days of harvest with the big straw stacks all proud and yellow in the fields; or the jingling sleigh rides in winter, and at the end putting the tramping, smoking horses into the hay-scented barn where the cows chewed their cuds in the dusky warmth.

But your great-grandparents had difficulties, too. Sometimes it didn't rain and the crops shriveled. Yet food still had to be bought for the children (your Grandpas and Grandmas), and food must be paid for with money. So Great-Grandfather might have had no present for Great-Grandmother at Christmas time — except his

love and perhaps some new pantry shelves she had wanted and which he cobbled out of some old, warped lumber. And in return, Great-Grandma might have knitted him a scarf with wool raveled out of old sweaters and socks — used wool, it is true, but still like new for warmth.

And the dust blew in summer and the blizzard in winter, and if Great-Grandfather had gone to town for supplies, Great-Grandmother set a lighted lamp in the window and sat up listening for the squeak of sleigh runners and the ring of harness bells.

Yes, your great-grandparents worked hard and had many disappointments, but if you were able to ask them about it, you would see a faraway look in their eyes, and they would gladly tell you of Nellie and Blaze, the Clydesdales, and what a faithful team they were; or of Spot and Heather and Blossom and how much cream they gave; or of the year Great-Grandmother raised such a lot of turkeys in spite of the coyotes.

And they would tell you of the shining ponds, which they would call sloughs, and of the wild ducks which quacked in them or darkened the sky as they flew into the stubble fields for their suppers.

And of the cold spells, when the prairie chickens fed around the barnyard like tame hens.

And how the meadowlarks sang in the spring, and the wild crocuses dotted the hillsides.

Your great-grandparents, and your grandparents with them, settled the prairies from Manitoba to Peace River, and that is a lot of country. They came from many

1

countries, from all over North America and all over Europe, and some of them didn't speak much English at first but today they are one people — Canadians.

So you may have heard Grandma telling about the lovely blouses *her* grandmother stitched when the family lived in Ukrainia. Or perhaps they came from Sweden, and Grandma has told you how the youngsters used to take the cows and sheep to the cool mountains in summer, while the grownups cut the hay in the valley below.

Or you may have heard Grandfather singing snatches of Scottish songs that fairly reeked of the mist and the heather, or have listened while he talked about the smell of wild thyme on the English Southdowns, from where you can look across the blue channel and see the distant shores of beautiful France.

If your name is MacDonald, you will know all about Prince Edward Island from Granddad's lips. If you are a McMillan, you may have heard about fishing and the fishing coves of the Maritimes.

But when your grandparents have finished speaking of Yorkshire pudding, maple syrup, and the gristmill at Melancthon (better try your atlas for that!), they will talk again about the homestead on which they grew up and of the clean winds and the great sunsets and the neighborliness. They will tell you how their mother — Great-Grandma to you — sent them off to school with a pat or a kiss and a ruby-red lard pail of sandwiches and apples. And how the teacher smiled from the school steps as she rang the after-recess bell. Or perhaps they will make you shiver by telling of the time a blizzard came up, and the phone was out, and they all sat around the school stove and sang, waiting for the men and teams to break through the drifts to take them home.

And how in summer they had to hurry home, scuffing the road dust as they went, for there were chores to do, cows to be brought up for milking, wood to be carried to the kitchen, or poultry to be fed.

This — all this — is a heritage you carry in your blood, in spite of changed times, in spite of the fact that most of you now live in the city.

You are the children of pioneers, and the heritage will not be denied, for you will want to pioneer each in your own way — perhaps here in our North, perhaps in distant lands, to help the people of other nations in Africa or Asia or South America.

I, too, am a grandfather.

I am one who came in earlier days and homesteaded on the flowery prairies. I saw and did everything of which I tell you, and because I like to draw, I have made pictures which will show you what pioneer life looked like.

You will see binders (they are not much used now) and horses — lots of horses — and threshing machines.

And because I hope you will want to draw too, I have left some pages blank. I used to get into trouble for drawing in books, and I know the temptation to doodle. So go to it!

Perhaps you will want to say where *your* grandparents' homestead was, or you may have an uncle or cousin still there.

You could make some little pictures of what you have seen in the country. Or if your parents have told you about something that happened on the farm, why not write it down. That way you won't forget.

Sometimes I'll ask questions to remind you of things, but you don't have to answer them! It's up to you, so have fun!

I hope this book will mean as much to you as it did to the grandchildren for whom I first made it.

Important note

There's something that you'll need to know and I forgot to put it in anywhere else, so I'll tell you here.

What is a homestead, anyway?

A homestead is (or *was* really, because there are hardly any left) a quarter section of unbroken land that you could have for free — if you lived on it and farmed for three years. The only payment was a small registration fee. In the early days, much of western Canada was given away in that way, because the government wanted the country to be settled and cultivated. It hasn't always been, you know.

A quarter section, in case you're wondering, is 160 acres, or about 64 hectares, not a very big farm by today's standards, but enough then, when everything had to be done the hard way, with horses and elbow grease.

So now you know about homesteads — read on, please!

January: Wood-cutting time

Cutting wood in the bluffs

Of course you have heard your grandparents say that, in their early days, there was no oil, gas, nor electricity for heating the farm houses. People who lived on the bald-headed prairies had to haul coal from the railway to keep their stoves going in the cold weather. But those who settled in the more wooded districts were luckier, for they had only to go to the bluffs (or groves) of poplar trees, where they could cut their fuel "for free."

The Nordals' homestead was near Saskatoon, Saskatchewan. Great-Grandpa Nordal was a good axman, for he had grown up in Norway, which is timber country. So he enjoyed going to "the bush," as they say, and cutting the loads of long, greenish poplar poles which would later be sawed into stove lengths.

To burn well, green poplar had to be cut, hauled, and sawed before spring and then allowed to dry all summer. So this work had to be done almost a year ahead.

January days are short and can be cold, so Great-Grandpa just went to the bush on the best days. When he was away, Great-Grandma Nordal usually did the farm chores, such as feeding the cattle and cleaning out the stalls. She always wore long skirts ("ladies" never wore pants!), but she tucked them up and out of her way when she went to work in the barn.

Great-Grandpa's wood-cutting was often interrupted by blizzards. After each storm, the trail to the bush had to be broken out afresh.

When it was very cold, the sappy trees froze hard, and Great-Grandpa had to keep his ax sharp. Also he had to be very, very careful, because the blade would want to glance off the hard trunk, and it might easily cut a leg or foot.

As each tree was felled, Great-Grandpa would cut off the top and trim the branches. Then, one by one, he would drag them to the bobsled and build his load. Then he threw a logging chain around the lot to hold them together and tightened the chain with a long pole called a "boomer." (You can see one in the picture on page 8.) Meanwhile the horses fidgeted about, longing to start for home, but when Mr. Nordal said "Whoa!" — loudly, like that — they knew better than to make off.

Wood-cutting looks like hard work today, but Great-Grandpa Nordal enjoyed it. He cut wood till he was past seventy, and he always said that, between this and keeping the water pump thawed, the winter soon passed!

I've drawn a picture of a pump for you on the preceding page. No one had water on tap back then, so it all had to be carried in buckets to the livestock and the house. Great-Grandma liked to say that the only time she had running water was when she was in a hurry and did the running herself!

Cutting wood in the bush.   R D Symons

Hauling home the poles

Great-Grandfather usually cut more poles in a day than he could haul home, so he piled the extra ones neatly by the trail he had cut through the bluff.

After he had enough wood cut for next winter's supply, it was Uncle Jerry who hauled those extra loads.

Here is Jerry when he was seventeen: a big, ruddy lad who never felt the cold. He liked to hunt, and from the top of the load he could easily spot deer tracks. Sometimes he took the rifle with him (but of course you aren't allowed to hunt deer in January now!).

Magpies often helped him, too, because these long-tailed birds would cry "Jack? Jack?" when they saw a deer in the bush.

Birdie and Robin, the little team of roan ponies, were small but strong. They could haul a big load quite easily when the trail was good, but after a strong windstorm, they had hard work plunging through the drifts.

In very cold weather, the prairie chickens used to burrow into the snowdrifts to keep warm, and when the sleigh passed close, they often flew up with a loud noise right under the horses' noses. Once this happened and the team tried to run away, but Jerry steered them into the deep snow, and the sleigh hit a stump. This stopped the team but upset the sleigh. Jerry had to crawl underneath the load to unhook the chain so he could unload the poles.

By the time they were loaded again it was getting dark.

Great-Grandma worried till Jerry got home, but then she only said to drive more carefully next time. She had a nice supper of roast moose ribs (Jerry's favorite) that she had kept hot for him on the back of the big, black cook-stove.

It is hard to say which enjoyed supper most after being out in the cold — Jerry, stuffing himself on meat and potatoes, or Birdie and Robin, munching hay in the dark barn.

January: your page

Have you ever seen someone cutting wood?

Did you ever ride on a horse-drawn sleigh?
Tell us about it!

I hope you can visit a farm this winter!

Do you think you can draw a magpie?

February: Deep-snow time

R D Symons

Stock at the straw stack

Great-Grandpa and Grandma Gilchrist lived in Manitoba. The province was settled before most of Saskatchewan and Alberta, so the Gilchrists had a well-established farm with good buildings at a time when people further west were still pioneers.

The Gilchrists had come from Scotland to take a homestead about fifty miles north of Oak Lake in Manitoba, near the present town of Hamiota.

They were grain farmers, in a small way, and also kept chickens and cows. The fine flock of Plymouth Rocks, with their neat black-and-white bars or stripes, was Granny Gilchrist's pride. There were always fresh eggs for breakfast, with bright yellow yolks to show they were really good for you, and a plump roast chicken with plenty of gravy for dinner on Sunday. Granny's flock was the best in the district, and she got top price for her eggs when she sold them to the storekeeper in town.

The Gilchrists also had horses, as our picture shows. Unless the cold was very bitter, the cattle and horses — except the work teams and milk cows — were allowed free run of the straw stacks all winter long.

These stacks were bulky — higher than houses — but were easily made. Every fall, at harvest time, the big steam threshing machine was hauled to the Gilchrists' farm. (Perhaps you've seen one at the museum. If not,

why not go when you have a chance?) The job of the threshing machine was to separate the kernels of wheat from the straw and chaff. The straw was then blown out through a long-necked spout, which could be swung about so as to make a cone-shaped pile that resisted the weather. There is a threshing machine at work, far in the distance, in the picture on page 55.

A lot of straw was wasted when the livestock wintered in the stacks, but straw was cheap and plentiful, and what the animals tramped underfoot made them a nice bed for the cold nights.

Sometimes the stock would eat into the stack until it got top-heavy, and great chunks loaded with snow would slide down and occasionally bury a cow. Or an old horse would get "cast" — that is, unable to get up from resting, because it had made a hollow in the soft, deep straw and could not get a grip with its feet.

Unless assisted such animals might die. So Mr. Gilchrist and the youngsters or Granny from her kitchen window had to keep an eye out for such accidents.

But for the children the best thing about a straw stack was the fun of climbing up and sliding down.

It was also fun when Great-Grandpa set fire to an old, half-rotten stack, and you could look from your window at night and see the sky lit up all red.

After the storm

The Tisdale district in Saskatchewan is what they call deep-snow country, and you may be sure that after a big snow- and windstorm, the drifts were really deep, so that neither man nor beast could get through them without shoveling.

The worst drifts were around the buildings, and sometimes it was quite a job to get out of the house and into the barn to feed the stock.

When the Clarkes homesteaded, it wasn't easy to afford lumber for building. They built everything with logs — house, barn, granaries, and chicken coop. These buildings were low, and when the snow got deep, they looked even lower; and when it drifted during a storm, there were times when you hardly knew the barn was there at all. It just looked like a big mound of snow.

And the snow would drift over the windows of the cabin and you couldn't see out, so Great-Grandma had to keep the coal-oil lamp lit — even in the middle of the day — until Mr. Clarke and the big boys had shoveled the snow away. (There's a lamp in the picture on page 74, just like Great-Grandma Clarke's.) Once the house door was free from snow, the men had to dig a path to the barns and shovel out the stable door.

One year the snow was drifted above the level of the eaves, and they made a tunnel to the door!

The barn would be very warm under all that snow, but, as it always turns cold after a storm, Great-Grand-dad did not shovel all the snow off the roof for fear the sudden change might chill the stock.

It would melt in spring anyway, and then the horses and cows would have to be kept in the corral, because the roof of poles and hay dripped water for a month and made the barn wet.

Great-Grandma had to do the milking outdoors then, with an old wooden crate drawn up to serve as a milking stool. But she didn't mind. She said the smell of sage blowing in off the prairie did her more good than all the spring tonics in the world.

The old log barn, which you can just barely see in the picture, is still standing, but it's in the shadow of a big, new one that was built later. The Clarkes use the old building for a workshop now.

February: your page

Do you know any horses by name?

Draw a barn if you like — I don't mind.

Have you ever shoveled snow?

Do you use a kerosene lantern when you go camping, or does yours run on batteries?

March: Odd-job time

Sawing wood for next winter

Now, with longer and milder days, it is time to saw up the poplar poles for next winter's fuel.

This picture shows *arrière-gran'père* Michaud (that's French for "Great-Grandpa") with his sons, using a buzz saw. They farmed near Lesser Slave Lake in Alberta, where most of the neighbors, like the Michauds themselves, came from French Canada.

Madame Michaud had died when Rose, the eldest, was fifteen, but Rose was a strong girl and able to keep house for the family. She quit school early to work at home, as it was common for young people to do then, because it took so many hands to run a pioneer farm.

Jules, the youngest boy, was a great hand at machinery. Because money was scarce and the homestead far from town, he had put his wits to work and made up this sawing outfit from bits and pieces. The old gasoline engine he had rescued from a dump!

Big Uncle Maurice usually fed the saw, *arrière-gran'père* threw back the cut wood, and Paul helped to hold the poles and push them along for each cut. But he had to take care he did not push Maurice into the saw blade.

Whenever the yellow sawdust got too deep and the pile of poles too far away, the saw had to be moved ahead with crowbars.

I haven't shown Rose, because she was in the kitchen cooking. I think she was baking bread — twelve loaves to a batch! If it had been Monday, she would have started the wash instead, with big tubs of steaming, sudsy water (which she got by melting snow) in the middle of the kitchen floor. She didn't have a washing machine, so it was bend and scrub, scrub and bend, up and down the washboard until the clothes were clean. Then came the heavy job of getting everything hung on the clotheslines outside. The clothes often froze in fantastic shapes before they were dry and came in stiff as boards.

There was even more to the wash-day chores than I've told you about, and it was all very hard work!

And always on the back of the stove, Rose had a simmering pot. That was dinner — pea soup and home-cured salt pork. M-m-m good!

When the men all trooped in at noontime, each would stand for a moment to say grace before a holy picture of the Good Shepherd.

"It is good to be thankful," said *arrière-gran'père* after dinner, as he stuffed his pipe with *"taba' canayen,"* his favorite tobacco. His brother Charles always sent him a big package each year from Trois Rivières. (You'll find that on your map.)

It took a lot of wood to keep the cookstove and the big heater fed. The pile of wood was between the house and the barn, and anyone coming in from milking or feeding the stock was supposed to pick up an armful for the house. This way, the woodbox was kept full.

Sawing Wood. Hope Springs Ranch.   R.D.Symons

Cutting ice

As March comes to an end, the weather can become quite warm, and then it is nice to work outside.

The hot summer season is approaching, and Great-Grandmother Macdonald wants lots of ice to keep her butter firm and her meat from spoiling. The butter is of her own churning, of course, and so much work to make — pounding up and down with the wooden dasher in the churn — that she wants to be certain it won't go rancid in the heat. There's a churn in the picture on page 41.

People often used to keep their butter in the cool darkness of the water well. But the Macdonalds had chosen a homestead by the shores of Last Mountain Lake, north of Regina, and one of the first things that Great-Grandfather Macdonald did there was to make an icehouse in the steep bank. It was a sort of cellar or cave, and in this he stored the summer's ice.

So you see him here on the lake, cutting the ice out in big blocks, while Eddie (who was sixteen then) loads them on the stoneboat drawn by Nancy and Ben. Eddie uses ice tongs for handling the ice blocks. They don't feel heavy in the water, but when they are out it takes all his muscle to heave them about.

See how low to the ground this stoneboat is. It's not really a boat, but a sort of sledge and is mostly used to drag heavy stones off the field.

If you look at the sky in this picture, you will see some geese going north. Great-Grandfather can hear them honking and thinks they have come too early, for they won't find any open water to settle on, except maybe on some rapids in the Saskatchewan River. It's usually April before they come, but the weather has been warm for the time of the year.

The farmers have a trail right across the lake-ice leading to Keddleston, but any time now, the lake may become unsafe for the teams. Great-Grandfather crossed last year on the tenth of April, but next day there was a big crack in the ice, and he was the last to do so.

Great-Grandfather and Grandmother Macdonald came from Prince Edward Island and knew all about water and boats and fishing, so they were happy by the western lake which contained so many whitefish.

March: your page

Les membres de la famille Michaud sont tous de braves travailleurs, n'est-ce pas?

Do you make ice cubes in the refrigerator?

Does your little brother puddle-duck around in the March thaw? Over the top of his rubber boots?

If you have read about Lorna Doone, you'll know they had sledges on Dartmoor just like our stoneboats.

April: Crocus time

Heather has twins

Spring was late that year. It was cold. Great-Granny Bradford had been worrying about Heather, her best Shorthorn milk cow. She wanted a fresh cow for spring butter.

Great-Grandfather said, "Don't worry. I've put her in the big box stall — not tied up — and I'll keep an eye on her. But why couldn't she wait for green grass to come? These early calves don't always do well."

"Heather's will," said Great-Granny in her dry way.

Well, days before Great-Grandfather expected it, something happened in the barn.

Mr. Bradford took his lantern one night (because Mrs. Bradford insisted) and went to the warm, dark barn for a last look around. He flashed the yellow light into the box stall and saw Heather with not *one,* but *two* calves!

One, a little white bull, was already on its feet having supper; the other, a red heifer, wet and droopy-eared, was lying down, while Heather mooed gently and licked it with her rough pink tongue to dry it off.

Great-Grandfather could hardly get to the house fast enough. "Nellie! It's twins!" he called out as soon as he opened the kitchen door. Mrs. Bradford looked up quickly, for this was the first of April, but she guessed that if he had wanted to fool her his voice would have sounded more sly.

"I thought it would be," was all she said, as she calmly lifted her knitting needles to the light to count the stitches, "but you don't need to shout, Albert. You'll wake Helen and the baby."

Great-Grandfather grumbled to himself. "*Two* early calves! Doesn't that beat all? Well, it's a sign of spring, anyway."

Helen, who was eleven then, was allowed to name the calves. First she thought of Pete and Repeat, but finally she decided on William Whitestone and Mary Redfern. She was an imaginative girl and read lots of books — including history.

25

Hauling rocks from the field

Great-Grandfather Smetaniuk homesteaded near Kamsack in Saskatchewan. He knew a lot about growing wheat, because he was born in Ukrainia, which is rather like our prairie land.

Last spring he had broken a plowshare on a great rock that was in the field. He had not hit it before because his plow had not gone deep enough, but in the course of time, the frost had heaved the boulder closer to the surface.

Although the summerfallow had not held the winter's snow and the soil was thawed by the middle of April, the ground was still too wet in the low spots for seeding, so Mr. Smetaniuk said, "Now is good time; we go fix that big rock."

He and Vasil, his son, took the biggest team and two strong logging chains and set out to tackle the monster. They also had shovels and crowbars.

First they dug all around the rock until they could get the chains on in such a way that they wouldn't slip.

Great-Grandfather was a calm, slow-moving man, and that kind of person is usually good with a team of horses. And so it proved, for when he picked up the lines and chucked easily to Ben and Tom, the Clydesdales, they leaned into their collars, took the strain and hung there.

"Use a little the crowbar," Great-Grandfather said to Vasil. And as his son bore down on the heavy steel bar, Mr. Smetaniuk chucked again to the horses.

You would have thought the harness would break, but no, the team took one slow, straining step, and the rock began to roll up out of its pit.

"Hold it," said Great-Grandfather to the team; and then to Vasil, "Get ready the crowbar." Vasil did so.

Grandfather chucked a third time. The team stepped up. The rock rolled out. And away they went to leave it at the fence corner.

"No broken plows this spring already," was all Great-Grandfather said.

April: your page

Do you like picking prairie crocuses?

Do you know a milk cow? What is her name?

Are *you* a twin?

How many stone piles do you see when you
take a drive in the country?

May: Robin time

Sowing wheat

Axel and Karl Brandt were brothers from Odessa (in Russia), but by blood they were German — some of the people the Empress Catherine of Russia had persuaded to settle near the Black Sea, long ago. (You may have to use your atlas again!)

They homesteaded side by side near Tramping Lake in Saskatchewan.

Great-Grandfather Axel married, but Karl never did. In this picture you see him seeding with a wide seed-drill and four head of Percheron horses — matched grays. These horses were his pride, more especially as he had raised them himself from a purebred mare that he'd bought cheap because she was lame from a wirecut.

Karl always liked drilling grain. He knew how to put the outside horse just *inside* the wheel track of his last round.

If you get a chance to see an old-fashioned seed-drill, you will notice it has smooth, wide steel tires on its wheels. These leave a good track in the soft soil and enable the operator to avoid missing a piece of land or seeding it twice.

It takes practice to follow that track when the dust is blowing, but the wise outside horse gets used to keeping beside it.

There is a step behind both ends of the drill for the driver to stand on, and he changes sides each time he comes to the end of the field. From the middle of the implement, he could not see the track, because the horses' heads would be in the way.

Meanwhile Great-Grandfather Axel has been harrowing to smooth out the drill marks; but he covers more acres per day than Karl does, and this gives him time after dinner to haul a wagon-load of sacked seed-grain out to his brother.

He stands the sacks at the end of the field, a few rods apart, and when the grain box on the top of the drill gets nearly empty, Karl dumps in a couple more sacks.

Each sack of a bushel and a half seeds just over an acre. "A bushel and peck" of seed per acre is a rule that Karl swears by. "The crop will root better," he says, as he starts down the field singing to himself. He sings, *"Fuchs, du hast meine Gänse gestohlen"* ("Fox, you have stolen my geese"), an old German song that seems to him to go well with the squeal of the drill.

Washing the blankets

The womenfolk were glad when spring came. The men were out in the fields instead of being underfoot, and Great-Grandma could get some of her bigger chores done.

Great-Grandma MacGregor came from Scotland, where they know all about wool and woolen cloth.

After she and Great-Grandfather Hugh came to Peace River, Alberta and started to homestead, one of the first things "Mistress MacGregor" got was a good supply of Hudson's Bay "point" blankets — heavy, thick, and brightly cross-barred with black and yellow, green and red.

These blankets kept the whole family warm all winter, even on nights when the wind blew and the fine snow sifted in around the doorjamb and through the cracks in the log cabin, leaving little drifts like cotton batting on the floor; or when the temperature went to minus forty or lower, and the horned owls hooted, and the trees cracked like the sound of a shotgun.

But after being on the beds all season, Great-Grandma's beautiful blankets would be soiled from smoke, and the nap would not stand up. So each spring they had to be washed and then put away against another winter.

Like Rose Michaud, Great-Grandma had no washing machine, but she was young and strong then and thought nothing of doing the heavy blankets by hand. In fact, she did them by "foot," tramping them in a big washtub.

Of course they could only be washed in the best of rainwater from the barrels that stood under the eaves. And they must go through several waters and not be heavily soaped or wrung out too much — just a little — and then be left to hang in the shade and drip. After that they could be put to flap in the sun and wind on the long clothesline.

Little Elspeth loved to carry the basket of clothespins and hand them up to her mother.

The big tree to which the clothesline is fastened is what they called a balsam poplar, or Balm of Gilead (you'll find that in the Bible). It has sticky, sweet-smelling buds in spring. Great-Grandma used to make these up in sachets, which she put in the big pine chest with the newly washed, fluffy blankets.

Nowadays we buy all sorts of things to make nice smells, but the old-timers always made do with things close at hand, and when the blankets were taken out for next winter, they smelled as sweet as sweet, and the nap was raised like new.

May: your page

Do you sow garden seeds in the spring?

Do robins nest in your garden? Why not draw us one?

How about helping Mother with those sheets or blankets? Or do they go to the laundry?

June: Raining time

R D Symons

Pulling out stumps

"Breaking" to a homesteader did not mean breaking dishes or toys. It meant plowing up or "breaking" new land, land that before had only grown wild things.

On the open prairies, about all that grew naturally were grass and flowers, so the farmer could get to work as soon as the June rains had made the ground soft. Also, at this time the grass was green and sappy, so that the sod, once plowed under, soon rotted — which was good. And yet it was sad to see the wild flowers bow their heads as they were buried so that people could grow food.

In the brushy districts, there were wolf-willow scrub to cut and groves of poplar trees to be removed. This made the job more complicated but it was necessary, unless you wanted a field like a jigsaw puzzle, which was hard to cultivate.

Of course, the larger bluffs were often left, and it was better so, for besides looking pretty (and being a good place for picnics!), they helped to break the hot, strong winds of late summer, which could dry out the grain heads too early.

So here we see Great-Grandfather Sorensen and his son Eric near Beaverlodge, Alberta, getting rid of a poplar bluff. First they cut off each tree about four feet from the ground. The poles would be used for firewood and fencing. But first the branches were trimmed off and piled, and in the picture you can see one of these piles burning.

When nothing was left but a number of tall stumps, Great-Grandfather brought Joe and Charlie, his oxen, all harnessed and dragging a long logging chain.

Then each stump was tackled in turn. First the men would take a shovel and dig around, so they could get at the side roots. These they would cut through with the ax.

Then the oxen would be backed up and the chain fastened to the top of the stump. Great-Grandfather would speak to them, and out would come that stump with a crackling sound as the tap root broke.

Sometimes a stump didn't want to come, and the men had to cut some more, and Tippy the farm dog would help by sniffing and scratching. Then Great-Grandfather would swing the team so as to pull from another angle. This usually did the trick, and Tippy would bark in glee as if he'd done it. Great-Grandma and the younger children, who had brought lunch out to the men and stopped to watch for a while, would laugh and cheer when the oxen finally lurched forward and the stump came free.

Riding the stag

I suppose the most famous name among makers of plows is that of Mr. John Deere.

The John Deere trademark, which was (and is) on every plow his company made, depicts a full-tined stag.

Among these plows was one specially made for breaking prairie sod, which is very tough. It had a seat for the rider, whose weight helped to keep it well in the ground. This type of plow was called a "sulky," after the sulkies which are used at the harness races.

Not that any races were run with sulky plows, especially when drawn by slow, placid oxen such as Great-Grandfather L'Heureux used at Jackfish, Saskatchewan, years ago.

There were "high lift" and "low lift" sulky plows, but the less said about the first the better. They turned over too easily if the lefthand (or "land") wheel hit a rock or an anthill. Then a big lever like the one that you can see in the picture would usually hit you just under the chin. And Great-Grandma, who knew all about first aid and home remedies, would have another bandaging job to do!

It was the famous "low-lift" sulky plow which was always called a "stag." That was a kind of joke, since most such plows were made by John Deere, and a stag is a male deer. There are still a few of these to be seen, but they are rusting in fence corners or behind old barns.

Mr. L'Heureux was not quite a son of Quebec but more of a grandson, for his parents had come from the Hudson Bay voyageurs and had themselves been born on the banks of romantic Red River. There was Indian blood in his family, too, as you would have been able to tell if I'd shown you his face. He was proud of his mixed heritage and of the name "Métis."

Great-Grandpa L'Heureux loved his oxen, which all had French names. They were called Onesime, Paul, Jean-Jean, and George, and he loved to sing old French songs to their plodding gait. Up and down the furrows they would go, *arrière-gran'père* and his patient friends, to the music of *"En roulant ma boule"* or *"Jamais je ne t'oublierai."* He could not sing *"Alouette,"* because his oxen walked too slowly.

But when it got too hot, so that even the gulls went back to the cool lake, or when the flies were extra bad, the oxen lagged. And even when Great-Grandpa shouted insults at Jean-Jean, the furrow ox, the animals heeded him not but left the furrow and, in spite of their master's orders, dragged him — stag and all — into the nearest slough.

Then the beasts would lie down in the shallow water to cool their flanks among the green grass and wild mint.

Well, Mr. L'Heureux (which means "happy one") simply lit his pipe, got over his "mad," and walked home to dinner!

June: your page

Did your Grandpa help his father pull stumps? Better ask him if you don't know!

Have you seen the oxen at "Pioneer Days" in Saskatoon?

Do you live near Lunenberg, Nova Scotia? You might see oxen there, too.

Sing "Alouette," why don't you, while you draw?

Dit-on: est-ce que votre grand-père est un fermier?

July: Butter time

R D Symons

Fencing the pasture

Great-Grandfather and Grandmother Northwind and their friends, the Yellow Blankets, thought they would like to go camping and earn some money at the same time, so they offered to build fences for their neighbor, Robert Craig.

Like so many Scotsmen, Great-Grandfather Craig was a great lover of good beef cattle. When he first homesteaded north of Lloydminster (look at the map again, please!), he wasn't sure whether he was in Saskatchewan or Alberta, but by the time he had built up his farm and his herds, his land lay partly in both provinces.

When herd law came in (which meant that cattle could no longer run loose on the prairie), Mr. Craig had leased some rough grazing land near the North Saskatchewan River, and so he was very happy to make a deal with the Northwinds and Yellow Blankets to fence it.

The Indians liked to work by contract — that is, for so much for a job — rather than for daily wages. The whole family came, with their ponies, wagons, dogs, youngsters, and all. Yes, those are their tents along the creek, and you can see the smoke of their cooking fires. While the men and boys and younger women worked on the fence, the older ladies looked after the small children and picked strawberries.

Mr. Craig had got them two bags of flour, a big bag of sugar, and had also killed a steer for them. The older women cut up the beef in long strips and hung it to dry on racks of poles. For supper, they will bake sweet bannock over willow twigs. They will put plenty of tallow in the bannock. They will also boil a pot of beef and make a big pot of tea, which they call *muskikiapway,* or "medicine water." After supper they will beat a drum softly and sing.

In the picture Johnny Northwind is in the wagon pounding fence posts, while his orphan cousin George Goosequill is making holes with a crowbar and setting posts in a straight line.

Meanwhile Great-Grandfather Yellow Blanket is sitting on a pile of barbwire spools, smoking his pipe. He is supposed to see that the work is properly done, but I think at this moment he remembers what fun it was to go hunting buffalo!

He does not hurry the workers. *"Wahpaki misawats ketwam kesekaw,"* he says — for tomorrow is another day.

This fence still stands today, although it has, of course, required many repairs since the pioneer days.

The milking corral

Lots of barbwire was used to make small pastures for cows and work horses on the homestead, but it was expensive, and sometimes the early settlers could not afford more than a couple of spools.

That is why Annie Swindahl had to herd the cows by day from June to September, when they might damage the crops if left to wander.

Annie missed some school, but she took her books with her; and, while the cows grazed on whatever they could find around the dried-up sloughs, she would lie on a knoll and do her sums, while the speargrass tickled her chin and the pipits sang in the brassy sky.

When the wind blew dust across the prairie, she would cuddle down behind a big rock.

Her father (Great-Grandfather Keetle Swindahl) had died of pneumonia, and Annie and her mother had to do their best without him. Kind neighbors seeded and harvested their crop — it was only fifty acres. But Mrs. Swindahl managed to make a living from her cows and chickens, for she was one of the best egg-wives and butter-makers in the district and had private customers in the nearest town which (as it happens) was Davidson, Saskatchewan.

She was also the best hand at making coffee and sweet cakes or bee-beer for picnics — a cool drink made with Manna Grana, which comes only from Sweden.

Annie couldn't herd cows at night, but her mother had managed to get enough wire for a milking corral. Into this the cows were driven at evening to be milked, and there they stayed all night and for milking next morning, after which they went out to graze again.

In this picture Great-Grandmother is saying: "It looks just like another dust storm coming up — ya! Hurry to house and shut vindows — ya, and take pussy with, or Blossom going to kick over mine pail."

The cows didn't like that big ginger cat. You can tell by the way they look at him.

Annie did, though.

She still remembers her farm pussy, for all she was a nurse at Saskatoon for years and years and is an old lady now — old enough to be your grandmother!

July: your page

Are you a Cree, an Ojibway, a Sioux, or a moonias? Which of these words means a white person?

Have you a cat? Is it pretty or ugly?

Try drawing a milk cow. You can put horns on her if you like — I don't very often. Some don't have any and some have them cut off!

August: Harvest time

Cutting grain with the binder

There are only a couple of places where you might see a binder today. One is in a weedy fence corner on the open prairies. Another is in one of the newer settlements in the North, where they are still occasionally used.

But when Great-Grandfather Boazman harvested his crop near Macklin, in western Saskatchewan, his binder and the horses that pulled it were his joy.

In case you don't know, I should tell you what a binder did. It had two jobs — to cut the grain and to tie it in bundles called sheaves.

After that, the sheaves had to be leaned against one another in stooks, with the heads up, so that the grain could cure. You can see stooks in the next picture. They're the tepee shapes.

Great-Grandfather never let anyone else ride his binder, so the stooking was left to his daughter and son, Jenny and Christopher.

When they saw their dad going proudly around the field, sitting up in the cool breeze, they looked forward to the day when they could do the same, instead of sweating on the hot stubble.

But they learned, like their father, that work is its own reward, and when at dusk they headed for the glow of light from the kitchen, it was with happiness that they thought of the good supper, with its smell of fresh bread, that their mother had ready for them.

Here you see the horses walking fast to get up quite a steep hill, for the Macklin district is a great rolling prairie, with good grain soil.

Sometimes the binder broke down — they used to quite a lot — or the twine which bound the sheaves would break and have to be rethreaded through the machinery. The horses liked this, for it gave them a rest.

The Boazmans had been landowners in the English Midlands but had never done much hard work there. They loved the prairie and did very well, in spite of the fact that they started in a sod shack which Great-Grandfather built himself. "A poor thing, but mine own," he used to say.

But if the house was humble, it was cheery, with Great-Grandmother Boazman's red geraniums, the bright calendars on the wall, and shelves and shelves of books about all the countries of the world, as well as one called *The History Of Israel and Judah,* which had been written by Great-Grandmother's brother.

Many years later, Jenny became a famous actress, and Christopher lectured in universities. The work was easier than stooking they found, but did not give as good an appetite!

Lunch in the field

Stooking is a hungry job, but it must be done! If the wheat sheaves were left on the ground as the binder dropped them they would soon rot on the underside; in fact, they would spoil all over if it were to rain.

So the sheaves had to be set upright in stooks, or shocks as they say in the States. These stooks were usually made of eight to ten sheaves, and if the binder-man had left the sheaves in a nice straight line (which is not always easy to do), then the stooks too would be in straight rows, which looked nice and was handy for the threshing teams which would come later.

The Porters, who farmed at Grande Prairie, Alberta, came from Owen Sound (that's Ontario). They had only one son, Jim. All the rest of the family were girls, and the Porters, who were a very "proper" family, did not think it was right for "young ladies" to work in the fields, though other girls in the neighborhood often did. So while Great-Grandfather Porter rode the binder (just like Mr. Boazman), a hired man, George Lorrie, helped Jim with the stooking.

They were the same age, and between the two they joked and told stories so much that Great-Grandfather finally put one on each side of the field to keep them apart. More stooks went up after that, for they wanted to meet at the corners to have a chat!

At harvest time Great-Grandmother always took a lunch to the field at four or five o'clock, for supper would not be until eight. She and one of the girls hooked a team to the buggy and took the coffee and cakes and fresh buns to the men.

We can see George turning over the buns to find the biggest. He used to provoke Mrs. Porter with his smart-aleck ways. But she was warmhearted and liked him, just the same, him being so far from home and all. She was sorry to see him go back to Ontario when harvest was over. Next Christmas George sent her a big jug of maple syrup!

Great-Grandmother had been a music teacher before she married Mr. Porter, and he had hauled her piano fifty miles to the homestead on a wagon when they first settled.

She taught all the girls to play, and they taught their children, and those children, in turn, are now teaching families of their own.

But Jim was no pianist. He liked machinery and finally left the farm to learn welding. This got him out of stooking, but the First World War came on (that was in 1914), and he joined the Canadian Army to fight in Europe. He did not come back, for his grave is in France.

August: your page

You must have seen a combine, at least. Why not draw one here?

Did you ever go with Mother to take a lunch to Daddy? Was it in a buggy or what?

Try drawing a picture of Daddy eating a bun!

September: Threshing time

R D Symons

Water for steam

Great-Grandfather Murray was a lover of steam engines. As a young man, he had fished off the east coast, making many trips to what they called "The Labrador," which is really the coast of Saguenay County, Quebec.

(Do look at the map again — it's fun!)

So he was familiar with all types of steam power, from little winch engines to the big boiler jobs. It was quite natural that after he left the sea and came west to take up land, he still thought about engines.

When he was established, he bought a great big steam tractor and a threshing machine (which he called a "mill") and set out to thresh his own and his neighbors' crops.

Now, steam engines need lots of water, and this is not always plentiful, especially in the country west of Moose Jaw, Saskatchewan, where the Murrays lived.

Water had to be hauled in tanks, often from quite a distance, and when I was young and worked for Mr. Murray, it usually kept at least two, if not three, of these tanks on the hop to supply the outfit.

Ask your Mommy or Daddy — if you don't know — why water is used up so quickly on a job like this. Or look it up yourself in the encyclopedia. It's interesting.

The man in the picture is Ted, who was Great-Grandmother's nephew. He was an orphan and had lived with the Murrays for years. So he really counted as one of the family.

Anyway, he was one of the water-tank teamsters. Here you can see him, about 1919, pumping water into his tank from a large slough. You can see the outfit threshing in the distance, and the plume of smoke and steam means that Great-Grandfather has given three toots on the whistle, which means he is running short of water.

I can't remember if Ted made it in time or if his wagon got stuck in the soft edge of the slough! His horses look big and strong, so I expect he was all right, don't you?

If you wonder why he is so far from the threshing machine, it is because he couldn't get up and down the steep bank of the slough any closer.

Supper for the threshing gang

There wasn't a better cook in the Simpson district of Saskatchewan than Great-Grandmother O'Reilly. You see, she got a job cooking in the shanties down East soon after she landed, as a girl, from Ireland.

It was in Ontario, too, that she met and married Big Pat, better known today as Great-Grandpa O'Reilly.

It was she who was "always wanting a bit of land, now; and a pig; and a place for the praties," as she called potatoes.

Pat was an easy-going creature and willing. So west they came in a "colonist car" on the Canadian Pacific Railway — hard seats, cook for yourself (on a wood stove right in the car!), and bring your own blankets.

As you see from my picture, they prospered, for they had the biggest house in that part of Saskatchewan.

Their son Mike had taken over most of the farm work, but Great-Grandfather still kept one hand on the reins, you might say, and did the gardening. He liked that, for on hot days he'd light his pipe and lie down on the cool ground between the potato plants.

Great-Grandma still made her famous pickles and preserves. People didn't have fridges and freezers, and they couldn't afford tinned foods, so everything had to be canned at home — vegetables, meat, fruit. First Great-Grandma spooned the food into jars or sealers. These she boiled for hours in a big copper canner on top of the stove. This was to kill the "microbes," she explained, meaning "bacteria."

Sadie — Mike's wife — did most of the cooking on the O'Reilly farm. That's her in the kitchen now.

It takes a lot of extra hands to do the threshing, and the O'Reillys were proud to feed the whole crew in the big dining room. They liked to show it off and had the idea that rooms are meant to be used, not shut up until Sunday.

Also, Great-Grandma couldn't abide a bunch of men crowding into the kitchen, not even to wash off the dust and dirt of the day's work. She set a big bowl, a pail of water, and a tin dipper on the bench at the backdoor, with a cake of homemade soap and a big roller towel, and here the men could splash and puff.

The men were always hungry. Work started at six in the morning and kept going till eight at night. Before and after work, they had their teams to feed and water.

The kitchen work started just as early and ended just as late, for the men had to be fed morning, noon, and night. At threshing time, Lena Statz from the next farm came in to help. Here she is setting a bowl of praties on the table, much to the admiration of young Nick, one of the threshing gang, who is on her left.

Great-Grandfather's cousin, Ned Day, is trying to crack a joke with Lena and doesn't hear Great-Grandma asking if he wants more coffee.

Mike is the big man at this end of the table.

September: your page

Have you ever noticed how the water in a tea kettle boils away? Where does the water go to, do you think?

Have you ever helped to serve at a church tea? Tell us about it, why don't you?

October: Market time

Country elevator

This is Great-Grandfather Phillips' sixty-bushel load of wheat being dumped in the first elevator built at Semans, Saskatchewan. Before this elevator was built, farmers had to get the Canadian Northern Railway Company to leave grain cars at the loading platforms that had been built alongside the track. It wasn't easy work loading the grain from a wagon into a boxcar with a big shovel.

And before that, before the railway line was made, they had hauled their wheat sixty miles with horses. That had meant stopping over for two or three nights, and Great-Grandmother, who stayed behind to mind the farm, used to bar the door when she went to bed. That was unusual in a homestead country; but then, she came from the East.

Ask Grandpa what it was like to ride a wagon over rough prairie trails for so many miles; ask him, too, how many pounds weight there is in a bushel of wheat, and you will agree that the new rail line and the new elevator were a boon indeed; for now the Phillipses were only seven miles from the elevator, and there was no shoveling to be done when they got there.

When the horses had pulled the wagon up the elevator ramp onto the scales, the elevator man simply weighed the load and then turned a crank. This lowered the back end of the wagon so that the grain fell through a grill into a pit below. From there a belt with cups on it, and operated by an engine, carried the wheat way up into one of the elevator's overhead bins.

I wonder why the elevator man always weighed the empty wagon before Mr. Phillips drove over the other side of the scales and out of the elevator.

When the elevator man wanted to load a train car, all *he* had to do was let the grain run down out of a spout into a boxcar on the track below. Easy!

Oh, yes, before he left, Great-Grandfather Phillips was given his grain cheque, which he could cash at the store — or take home to Great-Grandmother, who had a cracked teapot with bullfinches on it for a piggy-bank.

Both of them felt it right to grumble a bit at the price they had received and the number of pounds they had been docked (look in the dictionary!) for weed seeds.

Country store

This may seem a funny-looking store to you, after being used to supermarkets and things like that.

But Great-Grandpa Taylor thought it very handsome back in 1914 when he built it. He was proud of what he called his "Emporium." He was from the state of Michigan, where they used words like that.

Like most of my old friends, Mr. Taylor really came to Saskatchewan to take up a free homestead, but when he saw a new town going up he thought a store might be, as he said, "a better proposition than pushing a plow." (Of course, you don't really push a plow — the horses pull it; but Great-Grandfather Taylor was no farmer.)

He had many customers among the new settlers and did pretty well until the droughts and low prices of the 1920s, which were worse in the 1930s. Yet I must tell you that I never knew a customer to leave that store without some groceries, whether he had money or not. I ought to know, for I was one who sometimes had not. But he never told anyone, which is why I tell it now.

Most of the settlers were honest, and when they had no money, they brought produce to trade — chickens and quarters of beef and eggs and butter.

Once a woman brought in twenty pounds of butter in a carton and asked to speak to Great-Grandpa Taylor privately. She said, "You see, a mouse fell into the churn, but I fished it out. Only trouble was Dad and the boys knew, and said they'd not eat the butter; I churned anyway; couldn't afford to lose that cream. Now, if you'd trade me twenty pounds of somebody else's butter, no one will know and what we don't know doesn't fret us, see?"

Great-Grandpa agreed. He took the butter down to the cellar. Then he repacked the same butter in a different carton and gave it to the woman, who was happy.

He always loved to tell that story. "Two could play at that game," he'd say, "so everybody was happy."

After so many people left the land (what with people getting tractors and needing bigger farms), the store was closed. It still stands, with the paint on its false front all blistered and peeling.

This picture shows the store, but I couldn't draw Mr. Taylor, because he was busy and wouldn't keep still.

October: your page

Have you ever seen bread made? What does it smell like?

You could draw a picture of a supermarket if you like.

What is a false-fronted building, do you suppose?

November: Freeze-up time

Meat for winter

Prairie winters are long and cold, and it takes lots of good food to bring a family through, so the larder must be well stocked.

The Chandlers came from Tennessee and knew the old saying: "When you see a hog with a straw in his mouth, winter's purty nigh, an' you better go down south."

But the Chandlers couldn't go "down south" because they had lots of cattle and horses and pigs to take care of on their homestead near Moose Mountain in Saskatchewan.

The potatoes had been dug and stored, and Great-Granddad had been waiting for the weather to turn cold enough to butcher a steer and a couple of pigs, because he knew that eating lots of good meat with fat on it would keep you from feeling the cold.

A fall of snow and a heavy frost told him winter was coming on, and so in the picture you see a big steer hanging up. Maybe you've seen a carcass like that at the butchershop.

Great-Granddad, with a neighbor's help, has made a neat job. He has gathered up his tools and is taking a last look to see that the meat is out of the reach of dogs and cats. I had to draw it hanging too low, because I'm not allowed enough paper to show it as it really was.

Great-Granny Chandler (that's her red coat on the right) is taking the heart and liver to the house. She will stuff the heart and make milk gravy to go with the liver.

Tomorrow they will kill a pig, and then there'll be headcheese and sausages. Great-Granny will make them herself, and then she'll render down the fat to make lard. What a messy, smelly job that is — but you should taste the pastries and pies that Granny makes with her homemade shortening!

When the meat is all frozen outside, it will be cut up and stored in the granary, which is the only kind of deep-freeze they had then. They will haul it on that stoneboat you see with the hide folded up on it.

When the Chandlers first took the homestead, before they had much stock, Great-Granddad used to shoot deer with his old "spo'tin'" rifle, but later he gave that up for want of time. Besides, the government made it illegal to take deer except during hunting season, and Mr. Chandler had a great respect for the law and the Mounted Police.

Meat from the bush

Some of the men who came west to settle looked forward to adventure as well as farming. One of them was Olaf Steffanson, who came to central Alberta with his uncle and his cousin Oscar.

They were all from the Icelandic settlement at Gimli in Manitoba. And the Icelanders, true to their Viking blood, are an adventurous people, who first came to Manitoba in very early days, crossing the gray Atlantic in slow wooden sailing ships.

Olaf and Oscar were both eighteen, old enough to have homesteads of their own, and each took one in the same section as Great-Grandfather Steffanson, Oscar's father. Great-Grandfather was happy building up his farm, and so was Oscar, who soon married.

But Olaf remained a bachelor. He didn't like winter chores and longed for the bush country, with its solitude and the tracks of wild animals. So one year he went north of Cold Lake, Alberta and built himself a little hunting cabin in a spruce grove on the Martineau River. Here he went each year when the moose season opened in November, and here he stayed, sometimes for more than a month.

He was a good hunter and a crack shot and always got a moose. He used to leave his team and sleigh about thirty miles south of the cabin, because there was no trail the rest of the way. He had to rent a toboggan and sleigh dogs from an Indian friend to go on through the trackless bush to his cabin.

Frieda, who was one of his Indian friends, always took his moose hide in the fall, and in the spring she tanned it and made several pairs of moccasins and mitts. Some she kept for her work, but each fall Olaf was given a new pair of mitts and moccasins from the last year's hide.

He hated to go home in December. He had enjoyed the hunt. He had enjoyed the howling of the timber wolves and the hooting of the great gray owls.

He even enjoyed being all by himself in the dark, groaning forest. Some people would think it a lonesome life, but not Olaf. He was romantic and later wrote a book about the North.

Great-Grandmother was glad to see Olaf come home for Christmas with a load of good meat and his gun. Now he could shoot the coyote that had been taking her chickens!

November: your page

Which do you like best: beef, mutton, pork, or moose steak? Don't all speak at once!

Did your Daddy ever shoot a moose? Yes? Where did he get it?

If you like headcheese, tell us, please.

December: Holiday time

Shinny on the slough

When your Grandma and Grandpa were young and lived on the homestead, there were no cars for getting to town quickly and very few movies (even if you could get to them), and so people had to make their own fun and games.

Of course for the long winter evenings, there were plenty of good books to read, like *The Last of the Mohicans* and *Captains Courageous* and *Kidnapped* and *The Patrol of the Sundance Trail*.

And in summer the children could all go to the swimming hole in the creek after supper, and how they would play and splash and enjoy the cool water after the heat of the day and the walk back from school and the chores!

Then, too, there were gophers to trap, birds' nests to be found, and, on Saturdays, baseball.

But after all, the one great Canadian game has always been hockey, and lucky was the family who lived by a big slough.

The MacLachlans, near Red Jacket (Saskatchewan again!), had such a slough, and after it was safely frozen over the MacLachlan children — Margaret, Hector, and Hamish — would invite a bunch of neighbors to play.

But first they had to shovel off the snow, which was hard work, though they were too excited to notice.

Then, with cheap sticks or homemade ones, they'd play all day Saturday after chores, using what they called "road apples" (which were balls of frozen manure) for pucks. It never mattered if you lost one; there were plenty more!

They called their game "shinny," and children still play it when there aren't enough to make a team and for general practice, and many a first-class hockey player has learned the arts of the game this way.

It made the youngsters strong and ruddy, too; though, as Great-Grandfather used to say, "Och, now! If the callants could work as hard as they play, we'd not lack for gold whatever happened!"

Christmas on the homestead

Great-Grandfather Van der Putten knew more about tulips than wheat when he first took land at Botha, Alberta.

But Great-Grandmother knew a lot about cheese, and so when they got some cows, she started in with cheese-making, and between that and the pigs and some grain, they did pretty well, although cash was always scarce.

Great-Grandmother loved her Dutch dresser with its blue-and-white plates. *She* wasn't one to hide her good dishes away in a dark cupboard!

That's why the little house looks so cheery and shining.

Luckily, just before Christmas a man from the North came around one day selling small evergreen trees for seventy-five cents each. Great-Grandmother said, "I haven't much money, but would you take a nice little cheese for that tree with the broken branch?"

The tree peddler said he would, so the Van der Puttens got their tree, and, as you can see, once the broken branch was trimmed away, it looked very handsome. (The tree peddler was given a cup of coffee before he went.)

Tryntje, the eldest daughter (they called her Tina), made the cardboard and silver-paper angel at the top, and little Anna, the youngest, helped her big brother Jan to drape the tree with tinsel kept from last year.

Right now the family are singing round the tree. Soon they'll have their presents. There's a new pipe for Great-Grandfather, some knitting needles for Mrs. Van der Putten, and toys and books for the youngsters.

If you wonder where Great-Grandfather is, I must tell you that he's out feeding the stock, but soon he'll be in for the evening. He always said, "A merciful man is merciful to his beasts," and he will give his animals some extra treats tonight, for he remembers that it was a humble ox and a funny old despised donkey who first breathed on our Savior in that ancient stable long ago.

Jan is only fifteen, but you can see he is already taller than his mother!

December: your page

Is hockey *your* favorite game? Or would you rather read a book?

What books do you like?

Where are you going for Christmas? (To Grandpa's farm, I hope.)

Where on earth *is* Grandpa's farm? I've forgotten.

And now my book of pictures is finished
and I shall say:
Farewell to you,
grandchildren all!

Index

To find the page on which a particular family is mentioned, look under "Great-Grandma and Grandpa." You'll find a list of surnames there. For references to towns and cities in western Canada, check the entries for "Alberta," "Saskatchewan," and "Manitoba." Places outside of western Canada are listed under "Homesteaders, places of origin."

Author and painter R. D. Symons was born in England and emigrated to Canada in 1914. He homesteaded in Saskatchewan and began painting prairie landscapes and wildlife. The author of eight previous publications and a nationally recognized painter, Bob Symons died in 1973.